M000073199

Dedication

This book is dedicated to all of my students at Pearl-Cohn Entertainment Magnet High School, Nashville, Tennessee. They have inspired, challenged, and called me to a new level of love, hope, and belief in the impossible.

This book is also dedicated to my friend, brother, and intellectual peer Leon Harvey, Jr., who has served as the impetus for this and many of my intellectual and spiritual pursuits.

Special gratitude to the young people of the Temple Church for their willingness to believe in this journey when it was just an outline. Because of their belief, it has made it to this point.

Journey Towards Greatness

Foreword

Anyone can be great! Make no mistake, all of us. Dr. Martin Luther King, Jr. asserted that anyone can be great because anyone can serve. We all have the capacity to serve in some way. God calls and equips us with the ability to serve humanity, but we must be willing to do the internal work to either increase our service, or to discover what ways our gifts are needed for service in the world. The work I am referring to is an intentional effort to turn inward for a set period of time in order to focus on changing from the inside out. Our willingness to take this turn inward is the first step towards becoming great.

This notion of greatness I am referring to has less to do with fame, money, recognition, and notoriety, but more to do with self-discovery, increased spiritual insight, good judgment, creativity, and discernment. These qualities are only produced and nurtured through a process of communicating with God, and being honest with ourselves. For the most part, great plays, books, paintings, sermons, etc., are not produced overnight, but instead they are the products of deliberate focus, time, passion, and energy. For the next twenty-one days, I am inviting you to engage in a deliberate process or journey of focusing your time, energy, and imagination on not only what God has placed inside you, but also discovering how God may want to do something great through you! This journey will connect you to a broader sense of God in you. It will help you develop habits that can produce personal and spiritual fruit that will benefit you and those around you. Today represents an opportunity to start a new path, create a new song, write a new story, and discover a new truth.

A journey towards insight, wisdom, knowledge, and understanding can lead us to a place where hope, dreams, and ambitions are realized. For the **next twenty-one days** we will walk, talk, think, and commune with God in very intentional ways. This book is intended to help you deepen your relationship with God by engaging in the spiritual disciplines of reading, examining, reflecting, and praying. Each day will have a specific focus that will require us to read a passage of scripture, remember how the events of our past have shaped us, reflect on where we desire to be, and share and receive inspiration through prayer.

Hopefully by the time the journey is complete, we will have cultivated a deeper appreciation for spiritual discipline, developed a deeper sense of intimacy with God, and gained a better understanding of ourselves while discovering how we can use our greatness to make the world a better place! If you are still reading, then you are clearly ready to begin this journey. Let's go together!!!!!!

21dayjourneytowardsgreatness

DCD

Table of Contents

Prayer for structure, boldness, and openness

Prayer for a righteous mind, decisiveness, and energy

Prayer for passion, poise, and Godly priorities

Prayer for endurance, deliverance, and understanding

Prayer for inspiration, manifestation, and fresh
motivation

Prayer for transformation, sensitivity, and
accountability

Prayer for divine recall, protection, and interpretation

Prayer for renewal, hope, and new dreams

Prayer for consistent application, attentiveness, and
alertness

Prayer for justice, fellowship, and fruitfulness

Prayer for follow through, good judgment, and common sense

The Journey
Begins…

Day 1

Prayer for forgiveness, clarity, and insight

Opening Statement: Where we walk and who we choose to walk with has a tremendous impact on our progress in life. Today, consider what relationships and experiences in your life have given you a greater sense or understanding about the power of your story and why your story matters. It is possibly a story filled with mountains and valleys, good days and some days not so good; however, you have overcome many obstacles up to this point. Despite the injustices, problems, detractors and distracters, you are still here. Your being here today represents another opportunity for you to either discover or pursue your passion/s with strategy and prayer, with the belief that all of your experiences have equipped you for something great.

So hopefully today you begin a journey towards new possibilities, new ways of seeing yourself, and new ways of connecting to the God in you. And in doing so, I want you to consider the places and spaces you have walked in, through, over, and under. Consider the people who walked with you and those that walked away from you. Today is an opportunity to begin to walk a new way and talk a new way. If you want to grow, progress, leave a legacy, make a significant contribution to the world, better humanity, and sow seeds of hope, love, and power, let us begin a walk that can get us there!

Read: Psalms 1

Remember: Build your network in ways that support God's and your vision for your life. Ask yourself, "Which people in my network can solve this, connect me to that, inspire me, teach me, and challenge me?" The company you keep will determine if you will be a tree that produces fruit or one that withers. What does your tree look like? Look at your network and decide!

Reflect: On the lives of people who walked with God: those in the Bible and those the world will never forget. People such as Mother Theresa; Martin Luther King, Jr.; Mary McLeod Bethune; Enoch; Moses; Mary, the Mother of Jesus; etc. Think about the way they walked and talked and embodied divinity.

Prayer: God, before I can walk in the fullness of power, faith, clarity, discernment, insight, and wisdom, I ask for forgiveness. God, please forgive me. Please forgive those who have done me wrong, and forgive me for doing wrong to others, knowingly and unknowingly. Lord, make your will clear to me, and give me the insight to know which direction I should go.

Day 2

Prayer for power, discernment, and discipline

Opening Statement: Greatness comes from the most unlikely places and can happen to the most unlikely people. The life and times of Jesus is a narrative that reflects the reality that God works through those on the margins – giving power, insight, creativity, and faith to those who find themselves locked out and looked over. Identifying with Christ is to recognize the God of the "Ghetto", but it is also realizing that we are never out of the reach of God's amazing grace.

Wherever we come from or whatever has happened to us, we are still bound for something great. Often what many of us need is power, discipline, and discernment to handle the weight of our greatness. It takes courage to admit and accept the weight of greatness, but the good news is we are not left without instructions, reflections, and divine jewels that light our pathway, as we attempt to understand our own greatness while also appreciating the greatness in others. Today we look into the pages of wisdom to provide us with some harsh and hopeful truths that can help us handle the unique power we have been given.

Read: Ecclesiastes 1:1-15

Remember: Wisdom does not come to us without an intentional and intimate relationship with the All Wise; in order to gain wisdom we must be willing to do the spiritual work. Wisdom finds us as we seek her; she waits to see if we are serious enough to read, pray, study, think, serve, and meditate upon her, and if so we are rewarded with clarity, insight, creativity, discernment, etc. Is the journey worth it to you?

Reflect: Think about the wisdom you have already gained in your lifetime, and think about times when you were unwise and why. Now, consider at this very moment that you still have an opportunity to add knowledge and insight to what you already have and for what you are positioning yourself to gain.

Prayer: God, I believe that today is a day of power, a day to experience the radical reality of your miraculous and abundant grace. I will not forsake the opportunity to add knowledge to others and myself with the hope of encountering divine wisdom in the process.

Day 3

Prayer for creativity, humility, and patience

Opening Statement: Have you ever thought about how much creativity God has deposited in humanity? Look at buildings, cars, bridges, boats, paintings, instruments, jewelry, clothes, etc. Humanity continues to create, and this creativity is directly linked to a Creator who has given us the same ability to co-labor (with God) in the creation of our own future. We are gifted, talented, and creative beings, and because of those special gifts we can either create community or chaos. However, we must be humble enough to recognize our power, and patient enough to allow God to unveil the fullness of that power in due season.

Read: Philippians 1:6

Remember: If we believe that something has begun in us, we realize that there may be obstacles in our path. But the only reason we are still here is because God does have a plan for our lives. Our lives are purposed to show forth the glory of God in various ways. Today, be reminded that you have not come this far to give in, and God has not left you!

Reflect: On how many times you were ready to give up, and you just kept pressing your way. If you made it before, you have what it takes to make it again. You are not in the battle just for yourself but you are representing your family, friends, faith, and your future full of grace and favor. Hold on to your dreams, vision, and passion; God is not finished with you quite yet!

Prayer: God, give me the humility and patience to honor my creative genius. Let me not forget the source of my creativity. God, grant me the patience to cultivate my heart and mind in ways that are sensitive to the move of your creative spirit. Help me to create peace, power, love, hope, and reconciliation. Lord, I will always honor you for the power that will be shown through my creativity!

Day 4

Prayer for wisdom, knowledge, and peace

Opening Statement: Every journey requires trust in the divine directions we have been given, and trust in what we know about our past journeys. However, today, along the journey you are being invited to trust in God's word more than your own logic, education, or opinion. You are being invited to consider God's intimate knowledge of you, and how God has a plan to prosper you. You can have peace knowing that when you acknowledge God, God will protect, connect, and direct your path.

Read: Proverbs 3:1-31

Remember: You can trust God even if others have let you down (Mediate on V 5-6).

Reflect: How can/will I acknowledge God today? Am I willing to acknowledge God publicly? In what areas might I need to acknowledge God more? Make a list of areas in which you know you need to acknowledge God more (e.g., time, resources, reading the Bible).

Prayer: God, help me to trust you more in all areas of my life. God, help me to never forget to acknowledge you in all my ways. God, give me divine knowledge and wisdom.

Day 5

Prayer for courage and strength

Opening Statement: Today's journey invites you to consider what God has given you! How would you behave or face your fears if you knew you had access to power, stability, insight, and knew you were unconditionally loved by God? I am sure there are many answers; however, today you should be encouraged because you have access to a source of strength and courage that will keep on giving. The question becomes do you have the courage to believe it is yours?

Read: II Timothy 1:6-14

Remember: You have access to power in Christ that allows you to overcome your fears, strength that allows you to endure the testing of your faith, and love that can destroy hate.

Reflect: What area of my life do I need courage and power to reach my full God-invested potential (e.g., in school, on my job, in my community)?

Prayer: God, help me accept and believe in your spirit of power, courage, love, and stability. God, allow me to experience your divine love and transformative power which can allow me to face and overcome whatever obstacles might be in my way.

Day 6

Prayer for a sound mind, compassion, and renewed faith

Opening Statement: Along life's journey, we can and do get tired. And because life, like this journey, is a marathon and not a sprint, we must renew our minds, hearts, and spirits. On today's journey, you are invited to keep running the race but to also pause for some spiritual Gatorade that can replenish, revive, and rehydrate your faith.

Read: Isaiah 40: 28-31

Remember: Progress can be a slow process; however, if you are committed to the right process you will inevitably see some form of progress.

Reflect: I am running a marathon, not a sprint. I will seek to have a different mind because my race and my finish line are not like anyone else's. I have a lane that is just for me and I must run in that lane or risk being disqualified from the race.

Prayer: God, give me compassion for myself and others as we travel along this journey. Give me the mindset to stay the course no matter what. Give me the faith to believe and when my strength runs low or my eyes get heavy or my spirit is burdened, help me trust in your power to supply with me energy, passion, and focus to finish my course!

Day 7

Prayer for kindness, anointing, and favor

Opening Statement: The number seven represents completion; therefore, you should congratulate yourself for remaining on the journey for six days. Even if there have been challenges up to this point, I hope you are feeling and thinking differently, and if not, maybe you are reading today because you want to feel different or think differently. Today on our journey, we seek God's anointing or seal of approval on us and the work we have been assigned. Today we are in need of God's anointing to help us handle the tasks assigned to our hands.

Read: John 15: 13-17

Remember: The kindness we show to others is also a direct reflection of God's anointing and favor being upon us. God has put people in my life who show kindness and represent his favor.

Reflect: Jesus loved as a friend enough to give his best. Ask yourself, am I giving my best as a friend, believer, student, leader, father, mother, teacher, singer, etc.?

Prayer: God, I ask for divine favor over all of my friendships and relationships. God, I ask you to show me who my real friends are and anoint them with power, peace, love, and abundance.

Day 8

Prayer for vision, good partnerships, and meaningful connections

Opening Statement: Today, on the journey, you are invited again to look within to measure yourself. Before we hold others to a set of standards, we must make sure we are practicing what we preach. I'm not talking perfection, but I am talking about striving to do better after we have experienced the good and the bad. Therefore, today represents an opportunity to attempt to see things in a positive light throughout the course of the day no matter what happens. If you can do that for one day, your vision will change forever!

Read: 1 Corinthians 13:1-13

Remember: You reap what you sow and the question that we must always ask ourselves is, "Am I sowing good seeds daily? Am I sowing love, compassion, and hope in my relationships?"

Reflect: Think about the good/great connections and partnerships that have blessed your life. Speak the names of those who come to mind.

Prayer: God, grant me the vision to maintain good partnerships and help me to direct my resources towards doing what is just and fair on the earth according to the Law of Love. Help me to always appreciate the connection I have with you, amen!

Day 9

Prayer for love, increase, and new opportunity

Opening Statement: We are called to walk by faith, and our willingness to walk by faith is rooted in our love for God. Our walk may take us through dark and mysterious places, as well as green pastures. Whatever the case, our walk of faith may allow us to experience a tremendous increase in spirit, primarily because without faith it is impossible to please God. Thus when we live and walk by faith, it creates a new opportunity for us to experience a new dimension of God's essence in the spirit and in the world.

Read: Psalm 23

Remember: To find a quiet place (preferably outside) where you can walk and observe God's creation.

Reflect: As you walk today, think about God's intended plan for you to walk into opportunities, positions, and new beginnings. You are walking towards something. Remember, your past "**was**" (Read II Corinthians 5:17).

Prayer: God, thank you for being the good shepherd who has still prepared a table for us, a good shepherd who is supplying us with nourishment for the journey ahead. Lord, keep me with your divine tools (Rod & Staff) and I will be kept!

Day 10

Prayer for good stewardship, replenishment, and focus

Opening Statement: Where can we run in times of distress? Who is there to give ear to our plea? Who has prepared space to embrace our wounded souls?

The Journey continues!!! We are midway through this twenty-one days of intentional focus. I hope you are hanging in there and being challenged and blessed every day along the trip. Since we are almost at the halfway point, it is time for us to replenish and refocus so we can finish strong. Today, we want to focus on being comfortable in taking cover when God offers us refuge.

Read: Psalms 91

Remember: To focus on what you do have and not what you do not have. Remember you have life, a God who cares for you, and the opportunity to make a comeback or possibly a come up. Today, make a list of the good things you have in your life, and find a way to keep that list in a place where you can view it daily as a reminder that you may have more to be thankful for than you realize. Remember: I am protected, I am valued and valuable, I will march on anyway.

Reflect: God will not leave us without hope, even though we may face what can look like insurmountable odds. God still prepares a secret place for us to receive the power, the peace, and the strength we need to endure and overcome.

Prayer: Lord, I need a refuge, I need somewhere I can go lay my burdens down. Help me to keep my eyes focused on the spaces of refuge you provide. Help me share with others your divine restoration. (Find a quiet place to sit and commune with God.)

Day 11

Prayer for structure, boldness, and openness

Opening Statement: Today, along the journey, we are reminded that nothing great can be sustained without some structure or order. The God we serve is a God of order. As the people of God, let us be bold in our attempt not only to bring about structure in our personal lives, but also in a society that is in need of light, love, and divine liberation. Our boldness to speak truth, to believe God for the miraculous, and usher in a better world than the one we inherited, should only be tempered by our willingness to be humble and open to God's divine leading.

Read: I Peter 5:5-11

Remember: Our power lies in our ability to seek and submit ourselves to the will of God. While progress can be a slow process, today we are called to boldly declare our commitment to the God who will not leave us.

Reflect: To proclaim faith in God requires a bold spirit. This profession of faith allows us to have access to God and God's promises.

Prayer: I am no longer my own, but thine (John Wesley Covenant Prayer).
Put me to what thou wilt, rank me with whom thou wilt.
Put me to doing, put me to suffering.
Let me be employed for thee or laid aside for thee,
exalted for thee or brought low for thee.
Let me be full, let me be empty.
Let me have all things, let me have nothing.
I freely and heartily yield all things to thy pleasure and disposal.
And now, O glorious and blessed God, Father, Son, and Holy Spirit,
thou art mine, and I am thine.
So be it.
And the covenant which I have made on earth,
let it be ratified in Heaven.
Amen.
Read more:
http://www.beliefnet.com/columnists/prayerplainandsimple/201 0/02/john-wesleys-covenant-prayer-1.html#ixzz3LFtAG4RO

Day 12

Prayer for a righteous mind, decisiveness, and energy

Opening Statement: Today, along the journey, we are encouraged to examine our mental diet. We must ask ourselves if we are feeding our minds with the kind of spiritual nourishment (e.g., prayer, fasting, studying the word) that will help us understand God's will for our lives. Today we are being invited to make a decision to begin getting rid of those things that cloud, stagnate, or negatively impact our mind, body, and soul (e.g., food, people, technology, TV, etc.).

Read: Acts 3:7-8

Remember: The Holy Spirit has the ability to change our minds, give us the energy to accomplish what seems impossible, and purify us so that we bring divine power into all situations we face. The Holy Spirit has given us the ability to be transformers who, by virtue of word and deed, can change the circumstances around and within us. The question is do you believe in or want real change?

Reflect: The only thing we can give is what has been given to us through the Holy Spirit. We can start by asking ourselves, "What do I have to give? What do I have access to through the Holy Spirit? What can I give to my family and community as a result of the power from the Holy Spirit?"

Prayer: God, help me/us to use the power I/we have in You for good, help me/us never forget that you are the source of real power. God, please strengthen my/our bodies and minds so we may do your work of healing and promoting hope in the world.

Extra encouragement: Watch the movie *The Great Debaters* to more thoroughly stress the need for and power associated with a righteous mind and revolutionary thinking.

Day 13

Prayer for passion, poise, and Godly priorities

Opening Statement: Passion is defined as *a strong or extravagant fondness, enthusiasm, or desire for anything.* Today, on the journey, we are reminded that God was so passionate about our restoration that God sent His only son to die for our sins. The questions we are faced with today are: What are we passionate about enough to sacrifice for? Are we prioritizing passion so we can maximize the gifts, skills, and talents God has given us?

Read: Hebrews 12: 1-3

Remember: Passion without divine wisdom and understanding can turn into acts of hate, genocide, and destruction.

Reflect: If our passion drives us, we must be careful not to allow our passions to overrule our commitment or relationship with God.

Prayer: God, grant me insight, discipline, and poise to properly handle the power produced by my passion. God, let me not forget your priorities of love, faith, power, and strength as my passion opens doors and windows for me.

Passion Profile

Identify people in the Bible and others who were passionate and see what you can glean from them. For example, what can you learn from the life of David; Jesus; Paul; Mary, the mother of Jesus; Esther; Deborah; and people like Fannie Lou Hamer; Muhammad Ali; W.E.B. Dubois; Malcolm X; Martin Luther King, Jr.; Mary McLeod Bethune, and others.

For additional consideration in understanding and identifying your passion/s, consider an online assessment at http://www.thepassiontest.com/.

Day 14

Prayer for endurance, deliverance, and understanding

Opening Statement: Today, on the journey, look for examples of people who endured hardships not only for themselves, but for others. Think about the many things God has allowed you to endure and, as you think on these things, share with somebody how God has or is delivering you. Also consider what you have learned about yourself and God through some of those hardships.

Read: Proverbs 1:1-19

As you read, ask yourself, "What does it mean to obtain discernment?" (V5)

Ask yourself, "What is the relationship between the fear of God and knowledge?" (V7)

Ask yourself, "What is it that I know and understand now as a result of my experiences?"

Remember: God does not waste any of our experiences. The question is, were you paying attention to the life lessons being taught to you in those situations?

Reflect: How does the truth set me free? How is understanding more precious than gold or silver? How can I empower others with the knowledge and understanding I have? Do I believe I have something to offer from my experiences? What new piece of knowledge will I seek out today?

Prayer: God, give me the endurance to continue the quest for knowledge. God, help me to build and participate in the community in ways that speak of your power as the one who supplies wisdom and knowledge!

Day 15

Prayer for inspiration, manifestation, and fresh motivation

Opening Statement: Today, along the journey, we are reminded that we are creators like God because we are made in God's image. We are reminded that the Holy Spirit gives us the inspiration to overcome, restore, and engage in the realities that we face. Today we are reminded that, as long as we have breath in our bodies, God can make manifest something new in and through us.

Today we are reminded that we manifest whatever we give our thoughts to, so we must pay attention to what we think about. **Thought Inventory:** Make a list of the top five things that consume your thoughts most of the time. Consider if those thoughts are positive or negative. After you make your list, you will have a greater understanding concerning why you have or have not manifested the things you desire.

Read: Matthew 5:1-16

Remember: The light you have was not given by the world and cannot be taken away by the world. Today, remember that we must be in relationships that inspire and motivate us to get our shine on in the name of Jesus. Today, remember that your presence matters and you possess a great treasure working on the inside of you (2 Cor 4:7).

Reflect: Do I inspire others? Do I add value and flavor in my community, home, work place, or even in my church or place of worship? What is it that most inspires and motivates me; is it money, attention, cars, or clothes? Make a list of things and people who inspire you.

Prayer: God, help me to accept the responsibility I have to share my light with the world, not in a selfish way but in a way that honors the savior who always allowed His life to shine brightly everywhere He went. God, help me surround myself with people who motivate, inspire, and challenge me to reach my full potential in ways that bring glory and honor to your name.

Day 16

Prayer for transformation, sensitivity, and accountability

Opening Statement: Today, on the journey, we are mindful that time is filled with swift transition; therefore, we are called to be sensitive to the transitions constantly going on in the world—foreign and domestic wars, violence, police brutality, racism, ageism, sexism, classism, and other forms of prejudice and discrimination that divide us. Today we need God to transform our minds so we can challenge and change ourselves first and then become change agents in the world.

Read: Matthew 6:19-24

Remember: "Our deepest fear is not that we are inadequate but powerful beyond measure." – Marianne Williamson. Therefore, we must hold ourselves accountable to live each day fully with the faithful and steadfast knowledge and hope that God has equipped us with the ability to transform our/the world.

Reflect: On how we can show sensitivity to someone else who might need a listening ear, a shoulder to cry on, or just be a friend. When we are sensitive to others, we will reap the same sensitivity in our time of need.

Prayer: God of love and light, continue to show us the areas in our lives where we need to transform our minds so we are more accountable to your word and your people. Teach us, O God, to be sensitive to the needs of our families, communities, and friends.

Day 17

Prayer for divine recall, protection, and interpretation

Opening Statement: Today, along the journey, we are encouraged to look back and see where/how God has provided divine protection from dangers seen and unseen. Today we are encouraged to consider how we also have to protect our spirits and minds from the dangers of fear, apathy, and mediocrity. Today we are encouraged to think, "Is there something I think God is denying me? or have I interpreted God's delay as complete denial?"

Read: I Peter 2:1-10

Remember: God can provide us with divine protection as long as we remember, like the Hebrew boys, that even if God does not come when or the way we want Him to come, "God is still able." We are called to remember that even when we pass through the water or fire, we will not drown or be burned, says the Lord!

Reflect: Take time to consider that people's rejection of us might also be God's way of revealing who is really in our corner.

Prayer: Today we pray for divine protection over our hearts, minds, families, and communities. God, we pray for supernatural recall so we never forget your grace towards us. Allow us to recall how you have brought us over a way that with tears has been watered. God, we sing and speak your praises because you have kept us.

Day 18

Prayer for renewal, hope, and new dreams

Opening Statement: Today on the journey, think about dreams you have possibly realized and

think about dreams that have yet to reach the light of day. Today seek God's power to breathe new life into your dreams and aspirations. We can remain confident in knowing that God has not forgotten our hopes and can supply us the much needed energy and renewed strength to reach our goals and dream bigger dreams.

Read: I Peter 3:8-22

Remember: God is watching and we have been made alive by His spirit, which renews our ability to be agents of hope and help in the world. Remember you are not alone in your quest to become your best self, because God is standing close by. Therefore, we must remember that some days we are bridge builders and other days we are the bridge that serves as a platform to lift others up.

Reflect: What stops me from pursuing a dream? Who has tried to kill my dream/s? How can I feed somebody else's dreams? Who has fed my dreams? Write a thank you note to somebody who fed your dreams.

Prayer: God, help me to seek unity amongst humanity. Today, God, we need you to give us new dreams, renewed hope, and an unwavering commitment to seek your peace and power in our world.

Day 19

Prayer for consistent application, attentiveness, and alertness

Opening Statement: Today on the journey, we are called to pay close attention to our progress thus far. We are invited to remain consistent in applying God's word to build relationships, repair broken walls, and rebuild the areas in our lives that are in need of repair. What walls do you have broken in your life that need repaired (e.g., family, financial, communal, etc.)? Make a prayer list of broken walls/areas in your life that need repaired.

Read: Nehemiah 1:1-11

Remember: To let all your living be a consistent prayer, not just your words but even your breathing. Let your body, art, music, and other forms of creation serve as a reflection of your gratitude to a committed and loving creator.

Reflect: On how God has remained consistent in providing your needs.

Prayer: God, allow us to remain alert and consistent in the pursuit of purpose, with the intent of building self and others.

Day 20

Prayer for justice, fellowship, and fruitfulness

Opening Statement: Today, on the journey, we are called to be drum majors and majorettes for divine justice. Today we are faced with multiple challenges that pose a threat to justice and equality for all. Today we join in the fight for freedom, equality, and liberation for all of God's children. Allow your voice to be heard; allow your presence to be felt amongst those who have suffered injustice.

Read: Daniel 1: 8-21

Remember: Some things are only accomplished through sacrifice, prayer, and fasting. Sometimes our resisting food, TV, cell phones, and others things that command our attention can place us in a greater position to hear from God. Our discomfort during these times of sacrifice can also equip us to become the leaders we were destined to be. Your sacrifice for

God will never go without reward. The question is, what are you willing to give up in order to go up?

Reflect: In the life and times of Daniel, who, although captured in Babylon, did not conform to the rules of the culture, and because he sought to please the Lord he would receive God's divine favor. Today we observe Daniel's act of moral dissent as a testament to what the believer is called to do to represent God's kingdom even when it is unpopular, but we also use his example to see how God can and will deliver us when we take a stand for His truth.

Prayer: God, give us the courage to represent your name in perilous times. Give us the strength to unapologetically trust that you will honor our commitment to you. God, allow us to be a reflection of your power and might in the world as we seek to bear good fruit.

Day 21

Prayer for follow through, good judgment, and common sense

Opening Statement: Congratulations!!! If you are reading this page you have made it to day twenty-one. Although we have come to the end of this journey, there is still more road left to cover. However, take a moment to realize what you have accomplished over these past twenty-one days. As we/you reflect on the journey, we should also seek God to give us the will to follow through on the commitments, prayers, requests, and sacrifices we have made over these past twenty-one days. While this possibly has not been an easy journey, hopefully your mind has been challenged, your imagination expanded, your will fortified, and your faith strengthened during this process.

Your completion of this process reveals that you have the ability to complete a task. Hopefully, your completion of this process shows you how strong you are and how much God has in store for you. So on this day of transition, take time to thank God for the beginning of a great work in you and performing that work in you.

Read: Matthew 10:16-20

Remember: To intensively and intentionally guard your mind and your new-found freedom and strengthened faith. You are now a target for the enemy because you have completed this process and not everybody is excited about that. However, as a result of your commitment to this process, you will also have the opportunity to share your new-found wisdom and knowledge with those you never imagined.

Reflect: On God's ability to give you the words, energy, and insight to spread good news in the world. Reflect on God's grace and mercy demonstrated towards you throughout this process. Reflect on how much God desires to use you as an instrument of hope in the world. Reflect on how much God loves you, in that God would trade the garment of royalty and righteousness for sin and shame just to save, reconcile, restore, and sanctify you!!

Prayer: God, we thank and honor you for bringing us through this process. Now, O God, protect, strengthen, and guard our hearts so that we may continue to strive for Godly greatness. Give us the will to endure, the common sense to acknowledge your name, and the courage to stand on your word. God, we bless you for the opportunity to grow in grace and speak words of life and power to all. As we continue on life's journey, please wash us afresh in your spirit and give us clarity and divine consciousness as we seek to represent you now and in the days to come, amen!!!